THE LITTLE
ALASKAN
Salmon
COOKBOOK

FROM MY BOAT
TO YOUR TABLE

LADONNA GUNDERSEN

Photography by
OLE GUNDERSEN

Book design and published
by Ole and LaDonna Gundersen
Cover design
by Ole and LaDonna Gundersen
www.ladonnarose.com
www.facebook.com/ladonnarosecooks

Prepress and technical assistance
by Vered R. Mares, 𝕿𝖔𝖉𝖉 𝕮𝖔𝖒𝖒𝖚𝖓𝖎𝖈𝖆𝖙𝖎𝖔𝖓𝖘

First printing March, 2015
ISBN: 978-1-57833-612-8

Distributed by
𝕿𝖔𝖉𝖉 𝕮𝖔𝖒𝖒𝖚𝖓𝖎𝖈𝖆𝖙𝖎𝖔𝖓𝖘
611 E. 12th Ave., Suite 102
Anchorage, Alaska 99501-4603
(907) 274-TODD (8633)
Fax (907) 929-5550
With offices in:
Juneau and Fairbanks, Alaska
sales@toddcom.com
WWW.ALASKABOOKSANDCALENDARS.COM

Printed by Everbest Printing Co. Ltd., in Guangzhou, China,
through **Alaska Print Brokers**, Anchorage, Alaska.

CONTENTS

LET'S GET STARTED
Here's what we're about; why we wrote this book and the stars of the show
6

NIBBLES
Tasty starters from the ocean
13

SOUPS & SALADS
The living is easy and so are the recipes
27

BURGERS & SANDWICHES
Wild salmon tastes better; it's a fact!
39

MAIN DISHES
No fancy equipment or hard-to-find ingredients required
51

SWEET TREATS
Totally simple and scrumptious!
75

INDEX
84

Welcome to A

KETC

The Salmon C

SALMON

MARK

STOP

Gross-Alaska's
COLISEUM TWIN
THEATRE

2

SALMON

Jeep

aska's 1st City

IIKAN

tal of the World

SCANLON GALLERY

Arctic Spirit Gallery

SMOKED SAL

ALASKAN ART

Silver FUR GALLERY
KETCHIKAN

2 HR PARKING
8AM-5PM
MON-FRI

Let's Get Started!

The great thing about salmon is they represent summer; cooking and eating salmon is about as good as it gets. Friends, warm weather and the aroma of salmon caramelizing over a barbecue is glorious. Top it off with a wonderful dessert and you have pure bliss.

As a commercial salmon fisherwoman, I am blessed to have wild Pacific salmon readily available and have been eating this majestic fish for over two decades now. Through the years, when giving salmon as a gift, more often than not, people ask,

"What do I do with it?" and "How do I eat it?"

My goal with this book is to celebrate the extraordinary wild Pacific salmon and to help you cook salmon at home with pleasure and success. To me, that means being able to put terrific, delicious salmon dishes on my table without devoting a weekend to the preparation and execution of a meal. I wrote this book because I want you to enjoy the dazzling flavors of salmon and to be able to cook it as easily, happily and quickly as you make other favorite dishes for your table.

To accomplish this, I focused on everyday ingredients and recipes that would not take too much time and effort—salmon dishes you can make anytime, anywhere, quickly and easily. It's fun food, nothing too fancy, but it's all deeply satisfying. As you flip through the recipes, you will find classic favorites like Smoked Salmon Dip, Salmon and Cheddar Strata and Mini Salmon Burger BLTs as well as fresh ideas that capture the flavors of cuisines around the world, but have become familiar favorites because of their broad appeal. Some are quick and simple to prepare, others are a more labor of love - but all are delicious additions to a cook's repertoire of recipes.

I hope that what you gain from this book will not only be a great collection of recipes, but also a glimpse into the world of salmon fishing. When you venture to your local supermarket and you see the orange-red fillet of wild salmon, you will have a better understanding of how to prepare it and what it took to get it there.

Welcome to our world. I hope you brought your appetite!

–LaDonna Rose

THE STARS OF THE SHOW

PINK OR HUMPY SALMON

Average size is 3 to 5 pounds. Pinks are the smallest and most abundant of all salmon and mainly used for canning. Its delicate texture makes it suitable for dips, casseroles, patties and sandwiches. The name Pink comes from the pale color of their meat. As males approach the spawning grounds, they develop a large hump on their back, hence the nickname "humpy". Pinks run from mid-summer until early fall.

SOCKEYE OR RED SALMON

These sleek Ferraris of the sea average 5 to 8 pounds. Sockeye have a deep red meat, firm texture and separate into smaller flakes, making it attractive for hot dishes, soups and salads. Sockeye is the most versatile of all salmon and is available fresh, frozen, smoked and canned. Sockeye run in the spring to early summer.

KETA, CHUM OR "DOG" SALMON

Average size is 8 to 15 pounds - light in color, soft in texture and separates into large flakes. Often used for smoking and canning, making it especially suitable for appetizers and cooked dishes. Male chums develop large "dog" like teeth as they approach the spawning grounds, giving them the nickname "dog" salmon. Chums run in the mid - summer to late fall.

COHO OR SILVER SALMON
Average size is 6 to 15 pounds. Cohos are a very popular sport fish, due to their size and feistiness. The nickname silver comes from their bright shiny skin and tale. The flesh is slightly lighter red than Sockeye, separates into large flakes and is an excellent choice barbecued and in all dishes. Cohos run late summer to late fall.

CHINOOK OR KING SALMON
Kings are largest of the Pacific salmon - averaging 10 to 30 pounds, with some weighing as much as 70 pounds. They are prized for their superior quality, texture and delicious flavor, making them wonderful for barbecuing, roasting or mixed into a salad. Kings run in the spring.

Salmon are anadromous, meaning, they are born in fresh water, migrate to the ocean to grow into adults and then return to fresh water to spawn.

HEALTH BENEFITS OF
WILD PACIFIC SALMON

You have probably heard a lot about omega-3 fats in the news, but what exactly are they and why should you eat them? At one time, omega-3s were abundant in our diet. Now that we eat more processed and fast foods, most of us have become deficient in these important nutrients.

Wild salmon contains omega-3 fatty acids, which are understood to be important for our health. According to many research studies, omega 3s are vital for brain function, healthy skin and hair and a well tuned cardiovascular and nervous system.

Today, salmon is one of the ultimate health foods and one of the very best low fat protein sources available. A diet high in wild salmon may be your magic bullet for greater health and beauty benefits. When possible, choose wild salmon fresh, frozen or canned. It is superior to farmed-raised Atlantic salmon.

in order to discover new lands
one has to lose sight of the shore

We catch most of our food right off the back of our boat. As you might imagine, we eat lots of salmon, which is one of the best foods on the planet. I'm talking about wild salmon, not farmed salmon. Without grabbing my megaphone and climbing up on my soap box, I do need to say this. We have a saying here in Alaska:

"Friends don't let friends eat farmed salmon!"

Many salient health reasons exist, which a quick Google search will relay (including some of my own passionate crusading).

SALMON PARTY ROLL

Serves **4-6**

1 (6-to 7-ounce) **can salmon**, drained
1 (8-ounce) package **cream cheese**, softened
1 tablespoon **lemon juice**
1 tablespoon prepared **horseradish**
1 tablespoon **onion**, minced
¼ teaspoon sea **salt**
½ cup **pecans**, chopped
3 tablespoons fresh **parsley**, chopped

Combine salmon with the cream cheese, lemon juice, horseradish, onion and salt. Mix thoroughly.

Chill several hours or overnight.

Combine pecans and parsley. Shape salmon mixture into an 8 by 2-inch roll.

Roll in nut mixture. Chill well. Serve with crackers.

SMOKED SALMON DIP

Serves **4-6**

1 (8-ounce) package **cream cheese**, softened
¾ cup **sour cream**
1 tablespoon **lemon juice**
2 cloves **garlic**, minced
2 tablespoons **green onions**, minced
1 tablespoon fresh **dill**, minced
1 teaspoon prepared **horseradish**
½ teaspoon sea **salt**
¼ teaspoon black **pepper**
1 (6-to 7-ounce) **can smoked salmon** drained

Beat the cream cheese until smooth.

Add the sour cream, lemon juice, garlic, green onions, dill, horseradish, salt and pepper. Mix well.

Gently add the smoked salmon. Chill and serve with crackers.

SMOKED SALMON ON GRIT CAKES

Makes **12**

2¼ cups low-sodium organic **chicken broth**
1 tablespoon **butter**
½ teaspoon sea **salt**
¾ cup uncooked coarse-ground yellow **corn grits**
3 tablespoons **shallot**, minced
3 tablespoons fresh **basil** leaves, chopped
½ cup **Parmesan cheese**, grated
2 (3-ounce) packages thinly sliced wild **smoked salmon**

Mixed Berry Spread

½ cup **blueberries**, **blackberries** and **raspberries**
⅓ cup granulated **sugar**
½ teaspoon **vanilla** extract
½ cup **cream cheese**, softened
1 teaspoon grated **lemon zest**

Spray a 9 x 13-inch baking dish with cooking spray.

In a medium saucepan over medium-high heat, bring the broth, butter and salt to a boil. Gradually whisk in grits and cook 1 minute. Reduce heat to medium and simmer until grits are thick, whisking frequently, 6 to 8 minutes. Add the shallot, basil and Parmesan and cook for an additional 2 minutes.

Pour cooked grits into the prepared baking dish. Press a piece of plastic wrap directly onto the surface of the grits; refrigerate for two hours or until firm. Unmold chilled grits onto a large cutting board. Cut the grits into 12 (2¼-inch) cakes.

In a small saucepan over medium heat, combine the berries, sugar and vanilla and cook until mixture is thickened, about 8 minutes. Remove from heat and cool slightly. Pour berry mixture into a food processor and blend until liquefied. Strain through a fine-mesh sieve; discard seeds.

In a small bowl, using an electric mixer, blend together the strained berry mixture, cream cheese and lemon zest until well combined. Chill until ready to use.

In a large nonstick skillet over medium-high heat, sear each cake 2 minutes per side or until lightly browned and heated through. Remove from heat and cool slightly. Spread an even layer of the mixed berry spread onto each grit cake, then top with a slice of the smoked salmon, trimming salmon if necessary.

Garnish with a dollop of the mixed berry spread, a few berries and a sprig of basil.

PANCETTA WRAPPED KING SALMON KEBABS

Serves **4**
Rosemary Oil
¼ cup **olive oil** plus 1 tablespoon for grill
2 fresh **rosemary** sprigs
2 cloves **garlic**, thinly sliced
⅛ teaspoon crushed **red pepper flakes**

Salmon
¼ teaspoon sea **salt**
¼ teaspoon freshly ground black **pepper**
1½ pounds king, coho or sockeye **salmon**, skin and pin bones removed,
    cut into 1½-inch chunks
4 ounces **pancetta**, thinly sliced

Heat a grill or stovetop grill pan to medium heat.

In a small saucepan, heat the olive oil, rosemary and garlic over medium-low heat until the garlic sizzles and begins to brown around the edges, about 3 minutes. Remove the pan from the heat and stir in the red pepper flakes. Divide oil between two small bowls with a rosemary sprig in each and let cool to room temperature.

In a large bowl, combine remaining tablespoon oil and salmon. Toss to coat. Sprinkle the salmon with salt and a few grinds of black pepper. On a work surface, set out rows of 3 salmon chunks. Unroll pancetta slices into strips. Working with one chunk at a time, wrap strips once or twice around salmon. Skewer each row of salmon with chunks slightly separated.

Brush grill grate with oil. Place kebabs on grate, cook turning once, until fish flakes easily with a fork.

Place kebabs on plates and serve with rosemary oil.

SALMON SALAD WON TON CUPS

Makes **24**
30 **won ton wrappers**
1 tablespoon **olive oil**
2 (6-to 7-ounce) **cans salmon**, drained
½ cup **green onion**, chopped
½ cup **red bell pepper**, diced

Ginger-Lime Dressing
1 tablespoon **lime juice**
1 tablespoon low-sodium **soy sauce**
1 tablespoon **rice vinegar**
1 teaspoon **sugar**
1 teaspoon **ginger**, finely minced
1 teaspoon Thai garlic **chili pepper sauce** or your favorite hot sauce
1 teaspoon **sesame oil**

Preheat your oven to 325°F.

Lightly grease 30 mini muffin cups. Place center of won ton wrapper in wells of prepared pan to form a cup, allowing remainder of wrapper to extend above the pan. Bake in the oven 7 to 9 minutes, until crisp and lightly brown.

Whisk together all dressing ingredients in a small bowl and stir together well. Set aside.

Place the salmon in a medium bowl, add green onion, red bell pepper and the ginger lime dressing, stirring to combine. Drain off excess liquid.

To serve, spoon mixture into baked won ton cups.

A Note from LaDonna Rose
This is great with avocado!

MINI SALMON AND HERB QUICHES

Makes **12**

1 sheet **puff pastry**, thawed
1 (6-to 7-ounce) **can salmon**, drained
2 **green onions**, finely chopped
¼ cup **half-and-half**
⅓ cup **cheddar cheese**, shredded
2 **eggs**, lightly beaten
1 tablespoon **parsley**, chopped
muffin tin

Preheat your oven to 375°F.

Using a 3 inch cutter, cut out 12 rounds of pastry. Press into lightly greased muffin cups. Combine salmon with the onion, half-and-half, cheddar cheese, eggs and parsley. Spoon into pastry cases. Bake for 15 minutes or until golden and eggs are set.

A Note from LaDonna Rose
These delicious mini quiches are a wonderful party dish because they can be made in advance and then simply reheated before serving.

SPRING ROLLS WITH SMOKED SALMON

Makes **10-12**

3 ounces thin **dried rice noodles**
4 shiitake **mushroom caps**, sliced
2 tablespoons low-sodium **soy sauce**
12 round **spring roll wrappers**
2 cups thinly sliced **smoked salmon**
1 **cucumber**, cut into matchsticks (about 1 cup)
2 small **carrots**, cut into match stick (about 1 cup)
1 medium **avocado**, diced
1 cup **basil** leaves, coarsely chopped
1 cup **cilantro**, chopped
½ cup **red onion**, minced
½ cup plain **peanuts**, coarsely chopped

Dipping Sauce
1 cup rice wine **vinegar**
1 **green onion**, minced

Submerge rice noodles in hot water 8-10 minutes, until soft and clear. Drain and cut noodles into 2-inch pieces, set aside. Toss mushrooms with soy sauce in a small bowl, set aside.

Submerge one spring roll wrapper in a shallow pan or bowl of warm water for about 30 seconds or until softened. Remove it carefully, draining the water. Place it before you flat on the work surface. Arrange the smoked salmon slices, cucumber, carrots, avocado, basil, cilantro, red onion and peanuts in a log shape in center of wrapper. Lift the wrapper edge nearest to you and roll it away from you, up and over the fillings, tucking it in under them compressing everything gently into a cylinder shape, folding ends to seal. Set the roll aside on a platter seam-side down to dry.

Dipping Sauce: Combine rice wine vinegar and green onion in a small bowl.

Serve spring rolls whole or halved crosswise, with dipping sauce.

SOUPS & SALADS

VINTAGE-OF-THE-SEA CHOWDER

Serves **4**

4-5 large **potatoes**, peeled, diced
5 thick slices of **bacon**, cut into ½ inch pieces
5 tablespoons **butter**
¾ cup **onion**, chopped
4 cloves **garlic**, minced
¾ cup **red bell pepper**, diced
½ cup **carrots**, grated
¾ cup **celery**, diced
¾ cup all-purpose **flour**
6 cups **water**
2 (6-ounce) cans **clams** with juice
2 pounds (3-4 cups) **assorted seafood**, salmon, halibut, crab, shrimp
¾ teaspoon sea **salt** or to taste
½ teaspoon black **pepper**
1½ teaspoons **curry** powder
1 cup **half-and-half**
1 cup **milk**
1 tablespoon fresh **parsley**, minced

Boil potatoes until tender, drain and reserve. In a soup pot, fry the bacon until crisp. Using a slotted spoon, transfer to paper towels to drain. Add butter to the soup pot. Add the onion, garlic, red bell pepper, carrots and celery, sauté over medium heat until soft.

Stir in the flour. Pour in the water and clams with juice. Bring to a slow boil, stirring frequently, until thickened. Add the seafood, potatoes, bacon, seasonings, half-and-half and milk. Simmer until all of the fish is opaque throughout, another 5 minutes.

Ladle into warmed soup bowls and garnish with the parsley.

MUSHROOM, SALMON AND WILD RICE SOUP

Serves **4**

4 slices **bacon**, cut into ½ inch pieces
1 medium **onion**, sliced
1 **celery** stalk, thinly sliced
1 cup assorted **mushrooms** such as,
   button, cremini and chanterelle
2 tablespoons all-purpose **flour**
¼ teaspoon **Dijon** mustard
¼ teaspoon dried **rosemary** leaves
1 cup cooked wild **rice**
4 cups low-sodium organic **chicken broth**
1 cup **half-and-half**
1 (14-to 15-ounce) **can salmon**

In a soup pot over medium heat, sauté the bacon until crisp. Using a slotted spoon, transfer to paper towels to drain. Add the onion, celery and mushrooms and sauté until soft.

Stir in the flour, mustard and rosemary. Stir in wild rice and broth and bring slowly to a boil. Reduce heat to low, cover and simmer 10 minutes. Add the bacon, half-and-half, salmon and juice. Simmer uncovered, stirring occasionally until hot.

Ladle into warmed soup bowls and serve right away.

SALMON, CORN AND POTATO CHOWDER

Serves **4**

3 tablespoons **butter**
¾ cup **onion**, chopped
½ cup **celery,** chopped
⅓ cup **carrots**, grated
3 cloves **garlic**, minced
3 cups **potatoes**, peeled and diced
4 cups low-sodium organic **chicken broth**
¼ teaspoon sea **salt** or to taste
¼ teaspoon black **pepper**
½ teaspoon dried **dill**
1 (14-to 15-ounce) **can salmon** or about 1 ½ cups cooked flaked salmon
2 cups **half-and-half**
1 (15-ounce) can **creamed corn**
1 tablespoon fresh **parsley**, minced

In a soup pot melt the butter over medium heat. Add the onion, celery, carrots and garlic, sauté until soft.

Stir in the potatoes, broth, salt, pepper and the dill. Cover and simmer 20 minutes or until the potatoes are nearly tender.

Reduce heat to low and add the salmon with the juice, half-and-half and creamed corn, stirring until hot.

Ladle into warmed soup bowls and garnish with the parsley.

GRILLED SALMON CAESAR SALAD

Serves **4**

Croutons

3 ½-inch thick slices **French
bread**, crust removed and cut
into ¾-inch cubes
1 tablespoon **olive oil**
2 tablespoons **butter**, melted
3 tablespoons **Parmesan
cheese**, grated
2 large **garlic cloves**, minced

Salmon

4 (6-ounce) wild **salmon** fillets,
skin and pin bones removed
olive oil for grilling
sea **salt**
freshly ground black **pepper**

Dressing

2 large **garlic** cloves
3 **anchovy fillets**
½ teaspoon **lemon juice**
½ teaspoon Dijon **mustard**
½ teaspoon **Worcestershire** sauce
2 teaspoons **mayonnaise**
⅛ teaspoon sea **salt**, or as needed
¼ teaspoon freshly ground black
pepper
¼ cup **olive oil**

Salad

1 large head **romaine** lettuce,
washed, dried and torn into pieces
½ cup **Parmesan cheese**, grated
freshly ground black **pepper**

Croutons: Preheat your oven to 350°F. In a large bowl; combine the olive oil and butter. Stir in Parmesan cheese and garlic. Add bread cubes and toss until coated. Spread the bread in a single layer on a shallow rimmed baking sheet and sprinkle with a little salt. Bake about 15 minutes. Set aside.

Dressing: In a blender, combine the dressing ingredients until smooth.

Salad: In a large salad bowl, combine lettuce and croutons. Pour dressing over lettuce mixture; toss lightly to coat. Add ¼ cup of the Parmesan and toss well.

Salmon: Preheat a grill or stovetop grill pan to medium-high heat and lightly oil the grates. Season the fillets with salt and pepper. Grill the fillets skinned side up and cook 3 to 5 minutes. Turn fillets over and grill until fish is just cooked through, about 3 minutes more. Divide Caesar dressing among four plates and top with a salmon fillet. Garnish with Parmesan and serve.

VEGETABLE AND SALMON SALAD

Serves **4**
1 pint **cherry tomatoes**, halved
1 ½ cups whole **green beans**, cut into 1 inch pieces
1 small **zucchini**, thinly sliced
3 cups button **mushrooms**, thinly sliced

salad greens
2 (6-to 7-ounce) **cans salmon**, drained
fresh **parsley** to garnish

Dressing
¼ cup **mayonnaise**
¼ cup **plain yogurt**
2 tablespoons **sherry vinegar**
sea **salt** and freshly ground black **pepper**

Dressing: Combine the mayonnaise, yogurt and vinegar. Season to taste with salt and pepper. Set aside.

Put the tomatoes, beans, zucchini and mushrooms into a large bowl. Pour over the dressing.

Arrange salad greens on a serving dish. Add the vegetables and then the salmon.

Garnish with parsley and freshly ground pepper.

A Note from LaDonna Rose
This fresh-from-the-garden salad is one of our favorites!
It is light and can be made quickly.

SESAME SALMON SALAD WITH SUGAR SNAP PEAS

Serves **4**

¼ cup **rice vinegar**
3 tablespoons **olive oil**
2 tablespoons low-sodium **soy sauce**
1 tablespoon toasted **sesame oil**
1 ½ teaspoons **sugar**
1 ½ teaspoons fresh **ginger**, minced
2 (6-to 7-ounce) **cans salmon**, drained
1 cup **sugar snap peas**, sliced
2 **green onions**, sliced
6 cups **romaine lettuce**, thinly sliced
4 **radishes**, thinly sliced
¼ cup fresh **cilantro** leaves
1 tablespoon **sesame seeds**
sea **salt** and freshly ground black **pepper**

In a small bowl, whisk the vinegar, olive oil, soy sauce, sesame oil, sugar and ginger. Season to taste with salt and pepper.

In a medium bowl, combine 3 tablespoons of the dressing with the salmon, snap peas and green onions.

To serve, divide lettuce among 4 plates. Mound a ½ cup of the salmon mixture in the center of each plate and garnish with the radishes, cilantro and sesame seeds.

Drizzle with the remaining dressing, about 2 tablespoons per salad and season with freshly ground pepper.

BURGERS & SANDWICHES

CRANBERRY-ALMOND SALMON SANDWICH

Serves 2
1 (6- to 7-ounce) **can salmon**, drained
1-2 tablespoons **mayonnaise**
2 teaspoons dried **cranberries**
1 tablespoon **celery**, diced
1 tablespoon **carrots**, shredded
2 teaspoons slivered **almonds**
pinch of **cinnamon**, optional
4 slices whole-wheat **bread**

Combine the salmon, mayonnaise, cranberries, celery, carrots, slivered almonds and a pinch of cinnamon in a bowl.

Sandwich between two slices of bread and serve at once.

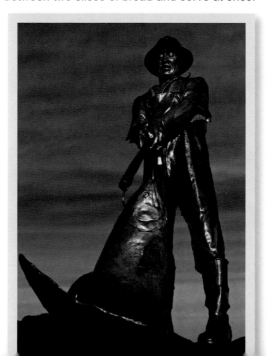

SPICY WILD SALMON SANDWICH

Makes 4

2 tablespoons **brown sugar**
1 ½ teaspoons **chili powder**
1 teaspoon ground **cumin**
4 (5-ounce) wild **salmon fillets**, skin and pin bones removed
1 tablespoon **olive oil**
2 teaspoons **jalapeños**, canned or fresh, chopped
½ cup **mayonnaise**
4 Kaiser rolls or **French bread**, split and toasted
crisp **lettuce** leaves
sliced **tomatoes**

In a small bowl, stir together jalapeños and mayonnaise. Spread on cut sides of rolls.

On a plate, stir the brown sugar, chili powder and cumin. Press tops of salmon fillets into spice mixture.

Heat a large skillet over medium-high heat until hot. Add oil, heat until hot. Add salmon, spice side down, cook 2-3 minutes or until browned. Turn salmon and cook another 3-4 minutes or until salmon begins to flake.

Place salmon on bottom half of roll, top with lettuce and sliced tomatoes. Cover with top half.

SMOKED SALMON CLUB SANDWICH

Makes 4

8 thick slices of **bacon**
½ cup **sour cream**
¼ cup **blue cheese** crumbles
1 clove **garlic**, minced
1 tablespoon Dijon **mustard**
1 tablespoon fresh **parsley**, finely chopped
1 **green onion**, finely chopped
1 pound **smoked salmon** (about 2 cups)
sea **salt** and freshly ground black **pepper**
12 slices **sandwich bread**, toasted
8 **lettuce** leaves, bib or green leaf
4 thick **tomato** slices

Fry bacon until crisp, drain on paper towels. While bacon is cooking, in a small bowl combine the sour cream, blue cheese crumbles, garlic, mustard, parsley and green onion.

Layer each of the 4 toast slices with ½ cup smoked salmon, another slice of toast, a mound of the blue cheese spread, 2 crisscrossed slices of bacon, 2 lettuce leaves, 1 tomato slice, a dash of salt and pepper and a third slice of toast.

Cut sandwiches into quarters.

SMOKED SALMON EGG SALAD ON GRILL BREAD

Serves 4

6 **hard-boiled eggs**, peeled
2 **green onions**, finely chopped
½ cup **celery**, finely chopped
1 tablespoon fresh **dill**, chopped
¼ cup **mayonnaise**, plus more for
  grill bread
1 teaspoon **sherry vinegar**
salt and freshly ground black **pepper**
1 (6-to 7-ounce) **can smoked salmon**, drained
sprouts, **lettuce** or watercress sprigs

Grill Bread
2 cups all-purpose **flour**
1 teaspoon **sugar**
1 teaspoon sea **salt**
½ teaspoon fast-acting **yeast**
½ cup **warm water** (105°-115°)
¼ cup **olive oil**, plus more for
  brushing
1 **egg**, beaten

Egg Salad: Place the eggs in a medium bowl and coarsely mash with a fork. Stir in the onions, celery, dill, mayonnaise and vinegar. Season to taste with salt and pepper. Gently fold in salmon. Set aside.

Grill Bread: In a large bowl, whisk the flour, sugar, salt and yeast. In a small bowl, whisk the water, oil and egg. Stir into flour mixture until a dough forms. Turn dough out onto a lightly floured surface and knead about 2 minutes. Put the dough into a lightly oiled bowl and let rest 10 minutes. Cut into 8 pieces. Roll each piece out into a 6-inch round. Lightly oil a large skillet and place over medium-high heat until hot. Grill bread rounds one at a time, turning once, until marks appear and bread is cooked through, about 1 minute per side. Keep bread warm wrapped in a cloth.

To serve, spread ½-teaspoon mayonnaise over each grill bread. Spread egg salad over the mayonnaise and top with the sprouts. Fold to close and serve.

LEMON SALMON BURGER WITH CREAMY BASIL SAUCE

Serves 4

1 (14- to 15-ounce) **can salmon**, drained
2 **eggs**
¼ cup fresh **parsley**, chopped
2 tablespoons **onion**, finely chopped
2 cloves **garlic**, minced
¼ cup panko **bread crumbs**
2 tablespoons **lemon juice**
2 teaspoons fresh **basil**, chopped
½ teaspoon dried **oregano**
⅛ teaspoon sea **salt**
pinch **red pepper flakes**
1 tablespoon **olive oil**
4 soft **hamburger buns**
4 crisp **lettuce** leaves
4 large **tomato** slices

Creamy Basil Sauce
2 tablespoons **mayonnaise**
2 teaspoons **lemon juice**
1 teaspoon fresh **basil**, minced

In a medium bowl, combine the salmon, eggs, parsley, onion, garlic, bread crumbs, lemon juice, basil, oregano, salt and red pepper flakes. Form into four patties.

Heat the oil in a large skillet over medium heat. When the oil is hot, add the patties and cook for about 4 minutes per side or until nicely browned.

Creamy Basil Sauce: In a small bowl, combine the mayonnaise, lemon juice and 1-teaspoon basil.

To serve, set the salmon burger on the bottom bun, a dollop of the basil mayonnaise, 1 lettuce leaf, 1 tomato slice and the top bun. Serve right away.

MINI SALMON BURGER BLT

Makes 10 patties

5 slices quality thick-cut **bacon**, cut in half

Salmon Patties

2 cups wild **salmon**, cooked, chilled, flaked

2 cups Panko **bread crumbs**, plus ½ to ¾ cup for forming

½ cup **green onions**, minced

½ cup fresh **cilantro**, chopped

4 **eggs**

3 tablespoons **lime juice**

3 tablespoons low-sodium **soy sauce**

2 tablespoons **rice vinegar**

2 tablespoons fresh **ginger**, minced

2 tablespoons **jalapeños**, canned or fresh, minced

1 tablespoon granulated **sugar**

1 teaspoon sea **salt**

¼ cup **sesame seeds**

olive oil for frying

Sauce

2 teaspoons **jalapeños**, canned or fresh, minced

½ cup **mayonnaise**

Burgers

10 **slider buns** or brioche rolls, toasted if desired split

crisp lettuce leaves, thinly sliced tomato, thinly sliced onion

Preheat your oven to 375˚F. Cook the bacon and drain.

Patties: In a large bowl, combine salmon through sea salt. Form mixture into ten patties; (⅓ cup each) packing each firmly. Press them into the remaining bread crumbs and sesame seeds. Place in freezer until just firm, about 20 minutes.

Sauce: In a small bowl, stir together jalapeños and mayonnaise. Heat 2 tablespoons oil in a large nonstick skillet over medium heat. Add salmon patties two at a time; cook until browned on both sides, turning carefully. Transfer the cakes to a plate.

Place the burgers on the roll bottoms and top with the bacon, lettuce, tomato and onion. Spread the roll tops with the sauce and place on the burgers.

SASSY SALMON BURGER

Makes 4

1 small **cucumber**, peeled and sliced
½ cup **sour cream**
2 tablespoons fresh **mint**, coarsely minced
1 clove **garlic**, minced
1 teaspoon **lemon juice**
sea **salt** and freshly ground black **pepper**
1 pound wild **salmon fillet**, skin and pin bones removed
1 large **egg** and 2 large eggs, hard-boiled and sliced
⅓ cup **green onions**, finely chopped
3 tablespoons **olive oil**
4 **soft buns**, or rolls split and toasted
12 fresh **spinach** leaves

Sprinkle cucumbers lightly with salt, let stand 10 minutes and then transfer to paper towels to drain. In a small bowl, whisk the sour cream, fresh mint, garlic and lemon juice. Season with salt and pepper. Set aside.

Slice the salmon lengthwise into ¼-inch wide stripes and then cut into ¼-inch wide pieces. In a medium bowl, whisk the raw egg with the green onions and ¼-teaspoon salt. Stir in the salmon.

Heat the olive oil in a large nonstick skillet over medium heat. Add salmon mixture in 4 mounds; gently press to form four patties. Cook 3 to 4 minutes. Carefully turn patties and cook without turning until done.

Divide the ingredients evenly, top the salmon patty with mint sauce, cucumber, sliced egg, spinach and top half of bun.

MAIN DISHES

SALMON AND CHEDDAR STRATA

Serves **4-6**

8 slices whole grain **bread**
¼ cup **butter**, softened
8 large **eggs**
1 teaspoon **brown sugar**
1 tablespoon Dijon **mustard**
2 ½ cups **half-and-half**
3 cups Cheddar **cheese**, grated
1 pound **smoked salmon** (about 2 cups), skin and pin bones removed
½ teaspoon **paprika**

Butter a 9 by 13 inch pan. Butter bread on both sides, stack the bread and cut it into small cubes.

In a medium sized bowl: whisk the eggs, brown sugar, Dijon and the half-and half.

Layer one half of the bread in the prepared pan, one half of the cheese and one half of the salmon. Repeat layers. Pour the egg mixture over all layers. Sprinkle paprika over the top. Chill overnight.

Remove Strata from refrigerator ½ hour before baking. Preheat your oven to 350° F. Bake for 45 minutes to 1 hour or until a knife inserted near the center comes out clean

A Note from LaDonna Rose
Fresh cooked salmon or canned salmon may be substituted for the smoked salmon in this recipe.

EGGS AND SMOKED SALMON IN A PUFF PASTRY

Serves **4**

1 frozen **puff pastry sheet**, thawed
8 **eggs**
½ cup **milk**
¼ teaspoon sea **salt**
¼ teaspoon ground black **pepper**
1 tablespoon **butter**
4 ounces **cream cheese**
2 tablespoons **green onion**, minced
1 teaspoon fresh **dill**, chopped
3 ounces thinly sliced **smoked salmon**
⅓ cup **Mozzarella cheese**, grated
1 **egg**, slightly beaten
1 tablespoon **water**

Preheat your oven to 350°F. Line a baking sheet with parchment, set aside. Whisk the eggs in a medium bowl until well blended, add the milk, salt and pepper. In large skillet melt butter over medium heat, pour in the egg mixture. Cook without stirring until mixture begins to set on the bottom and around the edges. Using a spatula, lift and fold the partially cooked eggs so the uncooked portion flows underneath. Continue cooking until eggs are just set. Remove from heat. Dot with cream cheese and sprinkle with green onion and dill. Stir gently until combined.

Unfold pastry on a lightly floured surface. Roll into a 15 by 12-inch rectangle. Place on baking sheet. Arrange the smoked salmon crosswise down the center ⅓ of the pastry, to within 1-inch of the top and bottom. Spoon the eggs over salmon and sprinkle with the Mozzarella cheese.

Combine beaten egg with water. Brush the edges of the pastry with the egg mixture. Fold one short side of the pastry over filling. Fold remaining short side over top. Seal top and ends well and brush the top of the pastry with the egg mixture. Top with 10-12 puff pastry stars, if desired and brush with egg mixture. Bake 25 minutes or until pastry is a lightly-golden brown.

CRÊPES WITH SMOKED SALMON

Makes **8**
Crêpes
2 **eggs**
1 ¼ cups **milk**
1 cup all-purpose **flour**
2 tablespoons **olive oil**
¼ teaspoon sea **salt**
1 tablespoon fresh **chives**,
  finely chopped
1 tablespoon fresh **dill**, finely
  chopped
nonstick spray

Filling
1 (8-ounce) package **cream
  cheese**, softened
3 **green onions**, minced
2 tablespoons fresh **dill**,
  chopped
1 tablespoon **lemon juice**
1 tablespoon **sour cream**
1 teaspoon grated **lemon zest**
¼ teaspoon black **pepper**
1 pound **smoked salmon** (about
  2 cups)
1 cup fresh **baby spinach**

Crêpes: blend eggs, milk, flour, olive oil and salt in a blender until smooth. Add chives and dill and pulse 1 or 2 times to just combine. Chill batter, covered 30 minutes.

Filling: Blend cheese, onions, dill, lemon juice, sour cream, lemon zest (grated lemon peel) and pepper in a bowl with a mixer until smooth. Set aside.

Stir batter to redistribute herbs. Heat a 10-inch nonstick skillet over medium heat. Spray bottom and sides with nonstick spray. Holding skillet off heat, pour in ¼-cup batter, immediately tilting and rotating skillet to coat bottom. (If batter sets before skillet is coated, reduce heat slightly for next crêpe.) Return skillet to heat and cook until crêpe is just set and pale and golden around edges, 10-15 seconds. Loosen crêpe with a heat resistant plastic spatula, then flip crêpe over gently with your fingertips. Cook a few seconds longer. Transfer crêpe to a wire rack to cool. Make other crêpes in the same manner, using nonstick spray for each one.

To serve, spread 2 tablespoons of the cheese filling on to top half of each crêpe. Top with 2 tablespoons salmon, then a few spinach leaves. Fold bottom half of crêpe up; fold again to make a triangle shape. Repeat with remaining crêpes and serve.

GARLIC-COCONUT SOCKEYE SALMON

Serves **4**

4 (6-ounce) wild **salmon fillets**, skin and pin bones removed
1 teaspoon **sesame oil**
2 tablespoons **olive oil**
¼ cup low-sodium **soy sauce**
1 tablespoon **honey**
2 teaspoons **garlic**, minced
2 teaspoons fresh **ginger**, peeled, minced
1 tablespoon **rice vinegar**
1 cup **green onions**, chopped

Garlic Coconut

1 tablespoon **olive oil**
¼ cup flaked **coconut**
1 tablespoon **garlic**, minced
sea **salt**

Salmon: In a medium bowl, whisk together the sesame oil, olive oil, soy sauce, honey, garlic, ginger, vinegar and half of the green onions. Place salmon fillets in a shallow baking dish and pour half the marinade over them. Refrigerate 30 minutes, turning once.

Garlic Coconut: In a small sauté pan over medium heat, add oil and coconut. Cook, stirring until coconut is golden. Add the garlic and cook 1 minute. Remove from heat and season with salt. In a small saucepan, heat remaining marinade mixture to a syrupy glaze, 2-3 minutes; remove from heat and set aside.

Preheat grill or stove-top grill pan to medium-high heat. Remove salmon from marinade and pat dry. Brush salmon with additional olive oil and grill 3 minutes skinned-side up. Turn and brush with reserved glaze. Continue grilling 3-5 minutes or until fish flakes easily when tested with a fork. Transfer salmon to a platter and brush with any additional glaze. Lightly press the reserved garlic-coconut on the top of each salmon fillet. Garnish with remaining green onions and serve.

SEARED SALMON WITH GREEN BEAN-RADISH SALAD

Serves 4

2 tablespoons **balsamic vinegar**
2 tablespoons **shallot**, minced
¼ cup plus 1 Tbls. **olive oil**, divided
sea **salt**
ground black **pepper**
4 (6-ounce) wild **salmon fillets**, skin and pin bones removed
½ pound **green beans,** trimmed or asparagus
1 cup **cherry tomatoes**, quartered
4 **radishes**, thinly sliced

In a medium bowl, whisk together vinegar, shallot and ¼ cup oil; season to taste with salt and pepper. Set aside.

In a pan of boiling water, cook the green beans until crisp tender, about 4 minutes.

Season salmon with salt and pepper. In a large nonstick skillet, heat remaining 1 Tbls. oil over medium-high heat; add salmon skinned-side up and cook 2-3 minutes each side or until fish flakes easily when tested with a fork.

Arrange green beans on 4 plates. Top each with a salmon fillet. Spoon vinaigrette over salmon; scatter tomatoes and radishes on top and serve.

HAZELNUT-ENCRUSTED WILD SALMON FILLETS

Serves **4**

½ cup **hazelnuts**
½ cup fresh **parsley**, chopped
1 tablespoon grated **lemon zest**
⅛ teaspoon sea **salt** and freshly ground black **pepper**
4 (6-ounce) wild **salmon fillets**, skin and pin bones removed
2 tablespoons **olive oil**
4 cups **mixed greens**
lemon wedges

Grind the hazelnuts in a food processor; do not over grind into a paste. On a plate mix the hazelnuts, parsley, lemon zest (grated lemon peel), salt and pepper.

Dry the salmon with a paper towel, dredge the fillets on both sides in the hazelnut mixture.

Heat the oil in a large skillet over medium-high heat, add the salmon and cook for about 5 minutes on each side until the fish flakes easily when tested with a fork.

Transfer to warm dinner plates and serve with mixed greens and lemon wedges.

BROWN SUGAR—GLAZED SALMON

Serves **4**

½ cup **butter**
½ cup **brown sugar**
salt and freshly ground black **pepper**
4 (7-ounce) wild **salmon fillets**, skin and pin bones removed
½ cup chopped **pecans**, optional

Preheat your oven to 400°F.

In a small saucepan; melt the butter and brown sugar. Whisk until combined. Set aside to cool.

Place the fillets skinned side down on a parchment-lined baking sheet. Season with salt and pepper. Brush the butter mixture over the fillets and pour remaining glaze over them. Top with pecans. Bake for 15 to 20 minutes or until fish flakes easily when tested with a fork.

Transfer to warm dinner plates and serve right away.

SESAME ROASTED SALMON

Serves **4**
Salmon
4 (6-ounce) wild **salmon fillets**, skin on and pin bones removed
2 tablespoons low-sodium **soy sauce**
2 tablespoons **sesame seeds**
1 **green onion**, finely sliced

Rhubarb Sauce
2 tablespoons **olive oil**
3 **cloves garlic**, minced
1 tablespoon **ginger**, minced
1 cup **rhubarb**, thinly sliced tossed with 1 teaspoon **sugar**
3 **green onions**, cut into 1- inch pieces
½ red **bell pepper**, cut into strips
1 teaspoon **jalapeños**, fresh or canned
2 tablespoons **Sweet Chili Sauce**
2 tablespoons **rice vinegar**
2 tablespoons low-sodium **soy sauce**
2 tablespoons **brown sugar**

Preheat your oven to 400°F.

Place the fillets on a parchment-lined baking sheet. Brush with the soy sauce and sprinkle with the sesame seeds. Roast for 15-20 minutes or until fish flakes easily when tested with a fork.

Rhubarb Sauce: Heat the oil in a large skillet over medium heat. Add the garlic and ginger, cook for 30 seconds. Add the rhubarb, green onions, bell pepper and jalapeños. Sauté 1 minute, reduce heat to low and add the Sweet Chili Sauce, rice vinegar, soy sauce and brown sugar. Cook to heat through.

To serve, transfer salmon to warm dinner plates, spoon rhubarb sauce over, garnish with green onion and serve right away.

LINGUINE, GOAT CHEESE AND SMOKED SALMON

Serves **4**

1 pound **linguine pasta**
8 ounces **goat cheese**, crumbled
6 tablespoons **butter**
3 cloves **garlic**, minced
3 **green onions** minced
½ cup white **cooking wine**
¼ cup flat leaf **parsley**, chopped
¼ cup fresh **dill**, chopped
¼ cup fresh **basil** chopped
2 cups **tomatoes**, chopped
2 (6-to 7-ounce) **cans smoked salmon**, drained (or fresh smoked)
sea **salt** and freshly ground black **pepper**

Bring a large pot of water to boil, lightly salt it, add the pasta and cook until al dente. Drain, reserving ¾ cup of the pasta cooking water.

In a large serving bowl, add the crumbled goat cheese.

In a medium saucepan, melt the butter over medium heat. Add the garlic and green onions, sauté 1 minute. Stir in the wine and cook, about 2 minutes. Add the parsley, dill and basil. Stir in the reserved pasta cooking water.

Add the pasta to the goat cheese. Pour the herb sauce on top, season with salt and pepper and toss. Add the tomatoes and toss gently.

Flake the smoked salmon on top, gently toss in and serve right away.

BAKED MEDITERRANEAN SALMON CASSEROLE

Serves 4

6 ounces **egg noodles**, cook al dente
3 tablespoons **butter**
½ red **bell pepper**, diced
2 cloves **garlic**, minced
¾ cup portabella or cremini **mushrooms**, sliced
1 (7-ounce) jar **artichoke hearts**, sliced
⅛ cup all-purpose **flour**
1 cup **milk**
1 cup **heavy cream**
2 (6-to 7-ounce) **cans salmon**, drained
3 **green onions**, thinly sliced
¾ cup **Parmesan cheese**, freshly grated
¾ cup panko **bread crumbs**
1 teaspoon **Italian seasoning**
sea **salt** and freshly ground black **pepper**
nonstick cooking spray

Preheat your oven to 350°F.

Melt the butter in a large saucepan over medium heat. Add the bell pepper, garlic and the mushrooms, sauté until soft. Stir in the artichoke hearts and the flour and cook for 1 minute. Pour in the milk and the heavy cream. Stir over low heat until the sauce thickens, about 5 minutes. Season to taste with salt and pepper. Remove from heat.

In a large bowl, combine the egg noodles, salmon, green onions, ½ -cup Parmesan cheese and the sauce mixture. Spray a 10-inch round casserole dish with nonstick cooking spray. Add noodle mixture and top with the bread crumbs, Italian seasoning and ¼ cup Parmesan cheese.

Bake for 20 minutes or until bubbly and golden.

FETTUCCINI WITH SMOKED SALMON

Serves **4**

1 pound **fettuccine**, cook al dente, drain and set aside
½ cup **butter** plus 1 tablespoon
4 cloves **garlic**, minced
1 cup cremini **mushrooms**, sliced
4 cups **heavy whipping cream**
1 (6-to 7-ounce) **can smoked salmon**, drained or fresh smoked salmon
¼ cup fresh **chives**, minced
sea **salt** and freshly ground black **pepper**
1 tablespoon fresh flat-leaf **parsley**, minced
¼ cup fresh **Parmesan cheese**, grated

In a small saucepan, melt 1-tablespoon butter over medium heat. Add the garlic and mushrooms and sauté until soft. Set aside.

Combine the cream and ½-cup butter in a medium saucepan. Cook and stir over medium heat until thick and glossy.

Add salmon, chives, garlic and mushrooms. Season to taste with salt and pepper. Stir gently for about 1 minute.

Transfer fettuccine to a warm serving platter. Pour sauce over and toss just to blend.

Garnish with parsley and Parmesan cheese and serve.

Rosemary and Garlic Roasted Salmon

Serves **4**

4 (6-ounce) wild **salmon fillets**, skin
   and pin bones removed
olive oil for grilling
sea **salt** and freshly ground black **pepper**

2 tablespoons **olive oil**
sea **salt**
freshy ground black **pepper**
2 sprigs **rosemary**, (about 2 Tbls.) strip the needles from the stems
   and finely chop
3-4 cloves **garlic**, minced
4 (6-ounce) wild **salmon fillets**, pin bones removed

Preheat your oven to 400°F.

Place salmon fillets skin side down on a parchment lined baking sheet.

Evenly distribute olive oil on each salmon fillet. Sprinkle salt and pepper over the fillets. Next, add the rosemary and garlic and lightly press into the salmon.

Bake for 15-20 minutes or until fish flakes easily when tested with a fork. Serve and enjoy!

SEARED SALMON WITH WILD BLUEBERRY SALSA

Serves **4**

4 (6-ounce) wild **salmon fillets**, skin and pin bones removed
olive oil for grilling
sea **salt** and freshly ground black **pepper**

Blueberry Salsa

1 cup fresh wild **blueberries**
½ cup crushed canned **pineapple**, drained
½ cup **red bell pepper**, minced
¼ cup **pine nuts**
¼ cup **red onion**, minced
¼ cup fresh **cilantro**, chopped
¼ cup **white raisins**
1 clove **garlic**, minced
1 tablespoon **lime juice**
¼ teaspoon **lime zest**
1 teaspoon **jalapeños**, minced
sea **salt** to taste

Salsa: Combine salsa ingredients in a medium bowl. Salt to taste. Cover and refrigerate one hour.

Salmon: Preheat a stove-top grill pan to medium-high heat and lightly oil the grates. Season the fillets with salt and pepper. Grill the fillets skinned side up and cook 3 to 5 minutes. Turn fillets over and grill until fish is just cooked through, about 3 or 4 minutes more.

To serve, place the salmon on a warmed plate and spoon blueberry salsa on top.

SWEET TREATS

Chocolate Mocha Baked Alaska

Makes **12**

8 ounces semi sweet **chocolate**, broken into pieces
1 cup **heavy whipping cream**
1 purchased **pound cake**, (about 14 oz.)
6 tablespoons **coffee liqueur**, (or 4 Tbl. strong coffee)
1 quart **coffee ice cream**
muffin pan
muffin liners
chill baking sheet in the freezer

Meringue
6 **egg whites**, room temperature
½ teaspoon **cream of tartar**
⅛ teaspoon **salt**
1 cup **sugar**
1 teaspoon **vanilla** extract

Heat chocolate and cream in a heavy small saucepan. Whisk over low heat until mixture is smooth. Chill 30 minutes until spreadable. Reserve extra ganache (icing) for plating.

Line muffin pan with muffin liners or pieces of plastic wrap, leaving overhang.

Prepare the pound cake, slicing it horizontally into four layers. Cut rounds from each layer; matching the size of your muffin pan openings.

Press ¼-cup ice cream into the lined muffin tin. Leave ½-inch space on top for the cake round. Pour 1-teaspoon liqueur (or 2-teaspoons coffee) onto each round, then spread with 2-tablespoons ganache. Place a cake round on top of the ice cream, ganache side down. Cover the pan tightly with plastic wrap and freeze until firm, at least 4 hours.

Meringue: Beat egg whites in a mixing bowl until foamy. Add cream of tartar and salt. Beat at medium-high speed until the whites hold a soft peak. Beat in the vanilla. Gradually add the sugar 1 tablespoon at a time. Continue beating until stiff glossy peaks form. (The meringue needs to be sturdy to form "insulation" and keep the ice cream from melting).

Assemble: Line the frozen sheet pan with parchment paper. Place the Alaskas on the parchment, cake side down. Quickly, remove the cupcake liners from the frozen ice cream. Generously cover each Alaska with 1 cup of meringue, spreading to form cloud-like swirls. Be sure the meringue reaches the parchment, creating a barrier so the ice cream doesn't leak. Place in freezer until ready to bake.

To bake: preheat your oven to 500°F. Take Alaskas directly from the freezer to the oven with rack in the top third. Bake 2 to 3 minutes just until the tips are lightly browned. If a little ice cream leaks, don't worry about it.

Carefully transfer Alaska's to chilled plates. Spoon warm ganache around dessert and serve.

MYSTERY BARS

Makes about **2 dozen**
40-50 saltine **crackers**
1 cup (2 sticks) **butter**
1 cup lightly packed light **brown sugar**
2 cups semi-sweet **chocolate chips**
1 cup **walnuts**, chopped

Preheat your oven to 350°F. Line a rimmed baking sheet with parchment paper. Place the saltine crackers in a row on the baking sheet, without any gaps.

Combine the butter and brown sugar in a saucepan and cook over medium heat until the mixture comes to a boil. Stirring constantly, boil for 3 minutes.

Spread the mixture over the crackers to cover completely. Bake until the caramel is bubbling, about 3 minutes.

Remove the baking sheet from the oven and quickly sprinkle with the chocolate chips, let them melt a bit and spread evenly around. Sprinkle nuts over the top.

Allow them to cool in the refrigerator for a few minutes before breaking apart into pieces.

CARDAMOM COOKIES

Makes about **2 dozen**

1½ cups (3 sticks) **butter**, softened
¾ cup granulated **sugar**
2 teaspoons finely grated **orange zest**
2½ cups all-purpose **flour**
1½ teaspoons ground **cardamom**
½ teaspoon sea **salt**

Using a hand or stand mixer, cream the butter and sugar on medium speed until well blended. Add the zest, flour, cardamom and salt. Turn the mixer on low speed and blend until the dough comes together in a ball. Shape the dough into a disk, wrap in plastic and chill for an hour.

Preheat your oven to 350˚F.

Line a baking sheet with parchment paper. On a lightly floured surface, roll the dough to a thickness of about ½-inch. Use a 2-inch cookie cutter to cut out circles of dough.

Place the cookies on baking sheets with about ½-inch between the cookies. Bake on the center rack of the oven until the cookies are lightly browned, 12-15 minutes.

Let the cookies cool before removing from pan.

COOKIE CRUST FUDGE PIE

Serves **4**

1 cup **butter**, softened
1 cup **sugar**
¼ cup baking **cocoa**
¼ cup all-purpose **flour**
2 **eggs**, beaten
1 teaspoon **vanilla** extract
1 teaspoon instant **coffee** granules
1 tablespoon coffee flavored **liqueur**
Pinch of sea **salt**
1 cup **pecans**, chopped
1 Oreo® **cookie pie shell**
Garnish: **whipped cream**, chocolate
   shavings or chocolate curls

Preheat your oven to 375°F.

In a large bowl, combine the butter, sugar, baking cocoa and flour.
Mix well. Add eggs, vanilla, coffee granules, coffee liqueur, salt and
pecans and mix well. Pour mixture into pie shell.

Bake for 25 to 30 minutes. Do not over bake; filling will not be firm
in the center. Slice and serve warm. Top with whipped cream and
chocolate shavings or chocolate curls, if desired.

A Note From LaDonna Rose
While fishing in Alaska, this is my go to dessert recipe. It's simple,
yummy and is our version of a big chocolate chip cookie.

BANANA CREAM PIE

Serves **4**

½ lb. **peanut butter sandwich cookies**, coarsely crumbled
¼ teaspoon sea **salt**
2 tablespoons **butter**, melted
2 **eggs**
1 tablespoon **rum**, optional
1 cup **sugar**
2 tablespoons **cornstarch**
1 tablespoon all-purpose **flour**
Pinch of sea **salt**
2 cups whole **milk**
2 tablespoons unsalted **butter**
½ teaspoon **vanilla** extract
3 ripe, firm **bananas**, quartered
whipped cream

Coat a 9" tart pan with removable bottom with nonstick spray.

Process cookies and salt for the crust in a food processor until fine. Drizzle in butter while machine is running. Transfer crumbs to prepared pan and lightly press to cover bottom and sides; set aside. Whisk eggs and rum for the filling in a small bowl.

Combine sugar, cornstarch, flour and salt in a saucepan, whisking to break up lumps. Gradually add milk and whisk until smooth. Cook over medium heat until thickened, about 8 minutes. Temper some of the hot custard into the egg mixture, then add the egg mixture to remaining custard. Continue to cook until thick and bubbly, about 3 minutes. Remove from heat.

Add unsalted butter and vanilla. Assemble pie by arranging bananas in the crust, cut side down. Pour filling over bananas and smooth to cover. Wrap loosely in plastic and chill overnight.

Serve pie plain or with whipped cream.

INDEX OF RECIPES

NIBBLES

Salmon Party Roll 14
Smoked Salmon Dip 15
Smoked Salmon on Grit Cakes 16, 17
Pancetta Wrapped King Salmon Kabobs 18
Salmon Salad Won Ton Cups 20
Mini Salmon and Herb Quiches 22
Spring Rolls with Smoked Salmon 24

SOUPS & SALADS

Vintage-of the Sea Chowder 28
Mushroom, Salmon and Wild Rice Soup 29
Salmon, Corn and Potato Chowder 30
Grilled Salmon Caesar Salad 32
Vegetable and Salmon Salad 34
Sesame Salmon Salad with
Sugar Snap Peas 36

BURGERS & SANDWICHES

Cranberry-Almond Salmon Sandwich 40
Spicy Wild Salmon Sandwich 41
Smoked Salmon Club Sandwich 42
Smoked Salmon Egg Salad on Grill Bread 44
Lemon Salmon Burger with
Creamy Basil Sauce 45
Mini Salmon Burger BLT 46
Sassy Salmon Burgers 48

MAIN DISHES

Salmon and Cheddar Strata   52
Eggs and Smoked Salmon
in a Puffed Pastry   54
Crêpes with Smoked Salmon   56
Garlic-Coconut Sockeye Salmon   58
Seared Salmon with Green Bean-
Radish Salad   60
Hazelnut-Encrusted Wild Salmon Fillets   62
Brown Sugar-Glazed Salmon   64
Sesame Roasted Salmon   65
Linguine, Goat Cheese and Smoked Salmon   66
Baked Mediterranean Salmon Casserole   68
Fettuccine with Smoked Salmon   70
Rosemary and Garlic Roasted Salmon   72
Seared Salmon with Wild Blueberry Salsa   73

SWEET TREATS

Chocolate Mocha Baked Alaska   76, 77
Mystery Bars   78
Cardamom Cookies   80
Cookie Crust Fudge Pie   81
Banana Cream Pie   82

Other Cookbooks by LaDonna Gundersen

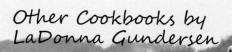

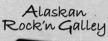

Alaskan Rock'n Galley

You'll Get Hooked On These Recipes Inspired At Sea!

LaDonna Gundersen

SALMON, DESSERTS & FRIENDS

LADONNA GUNDERSEN

author of Alaskan Rock'n Galley

INCLUDES OVER 24 CANNED SALMON RECIPES!

YOUR COMPLETE GUIDE TO UNDERSTANDING, SELECTING AND ENJOYING THE WILD PACIFIC SALMON

PHOTOGRAPHS BY OLE GUNDERSEN

My Tiny Alaskan Oven

Simple Scrumptious Recipes for Busy People

AUTHOR OF SALMON, DESSERTS & FRIENDS
LADONNA ROSE GUNDERSEN

photography by Ole Gundersen